Keep On Kicking

That's My Plan

By Jerry Horton

WestBow Press books may be ordered through booksellers or by contacting:

WestBow Press
A Division of Thomas Nelson & Zondervan
1663 Liberty Drive
Bloomington, IN 47403
www.westbowpress.com
844-714-3454

ISBN: 979-8-3850-4400-9 (sc)
ISBN: 979-8-3850-4399-6 (e)

Print information available on the last page.

WestBow Press rev. date: 03/19/2025

Contents

Dedication

This book is dedicated to Dr. John Caylor Jr., who served as my campus minister, while I attended West Georgia College in the mid 1970's. I will never forget the fall evening, as a freshmen, when Mr. Caylor, gave a brief message on the importance of working through the difficulties during our college days, and the days after our graduation from college. He closed his message by reciting the story you are about to read.

I put the story to memory and over the years re-editing it to my southern vernacular.

This book is also dedicated to my children who have heard me recite the story so many times they can repeat it, word for word, with me. And to my wife Carol, who through life's difficulties, has never given up, but is still churning butter!

Lastly, this book is dedicated to all who struggle with life's difficulties and reach the point of wanting to give up. To all of you, please read this story to yourself and keep on kicking!

Foreword

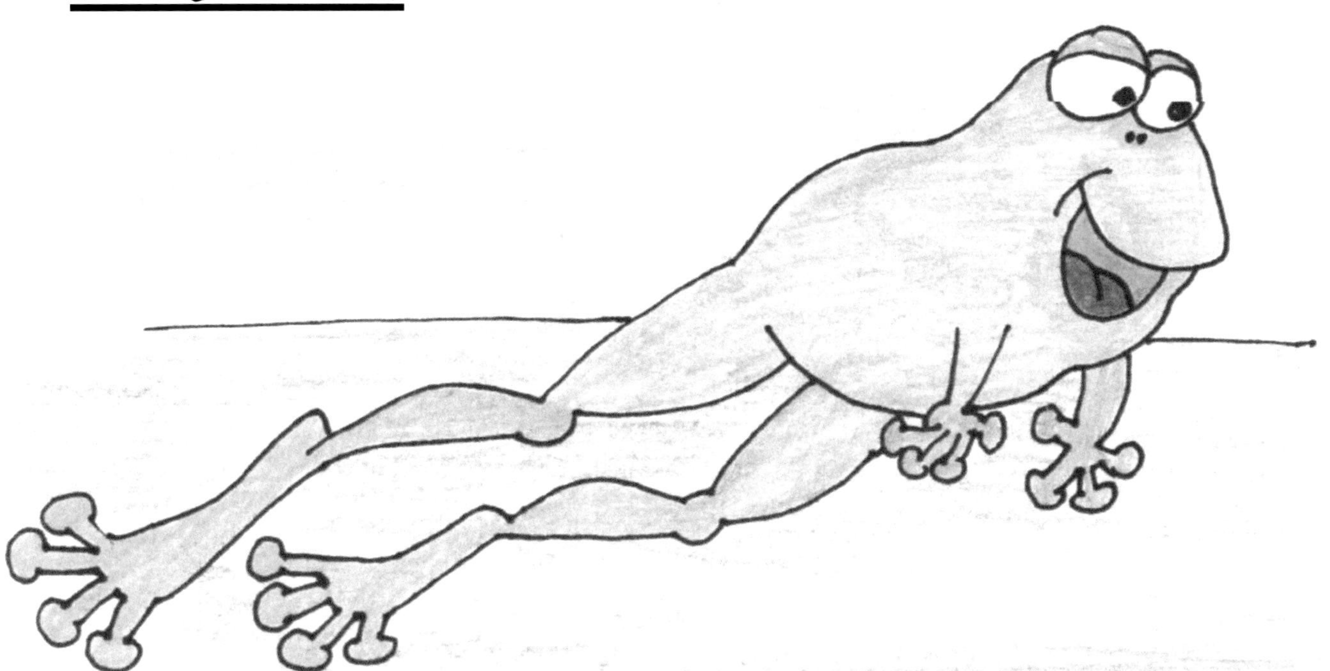

The word "forward", can be an order or a focused desire, that motivates a person to move on in a positive direction. It is such a motivating word that 18 books of the Bible and 46 different verses reference moving forward. Sometimes our past and present circumstances and our unknown future may cause us to think about giving up even before we try to move forward.

This simple book is a poetic retelling of an old Russian folk tale, from a Georgia boy's perspective. It's about two frogs who find themselves in a trying situation. It is meant to be an encouragement for you to move forward, to keep on kicking!

Two bright young frogs from inland bogs

had spent the night in drinking.

As morning broke
and they awoke,
while yet their eyes were blinking.

A farmer's pail came to the swell, and caught them quick as winking.

'Ere they could gather scattered senses,

or breathe a prayer for past offences.

The farmer fast, hard working man had
dumped them in the milkman's can.

The can filled up and the cover went down.
And sooner, they started off to town.

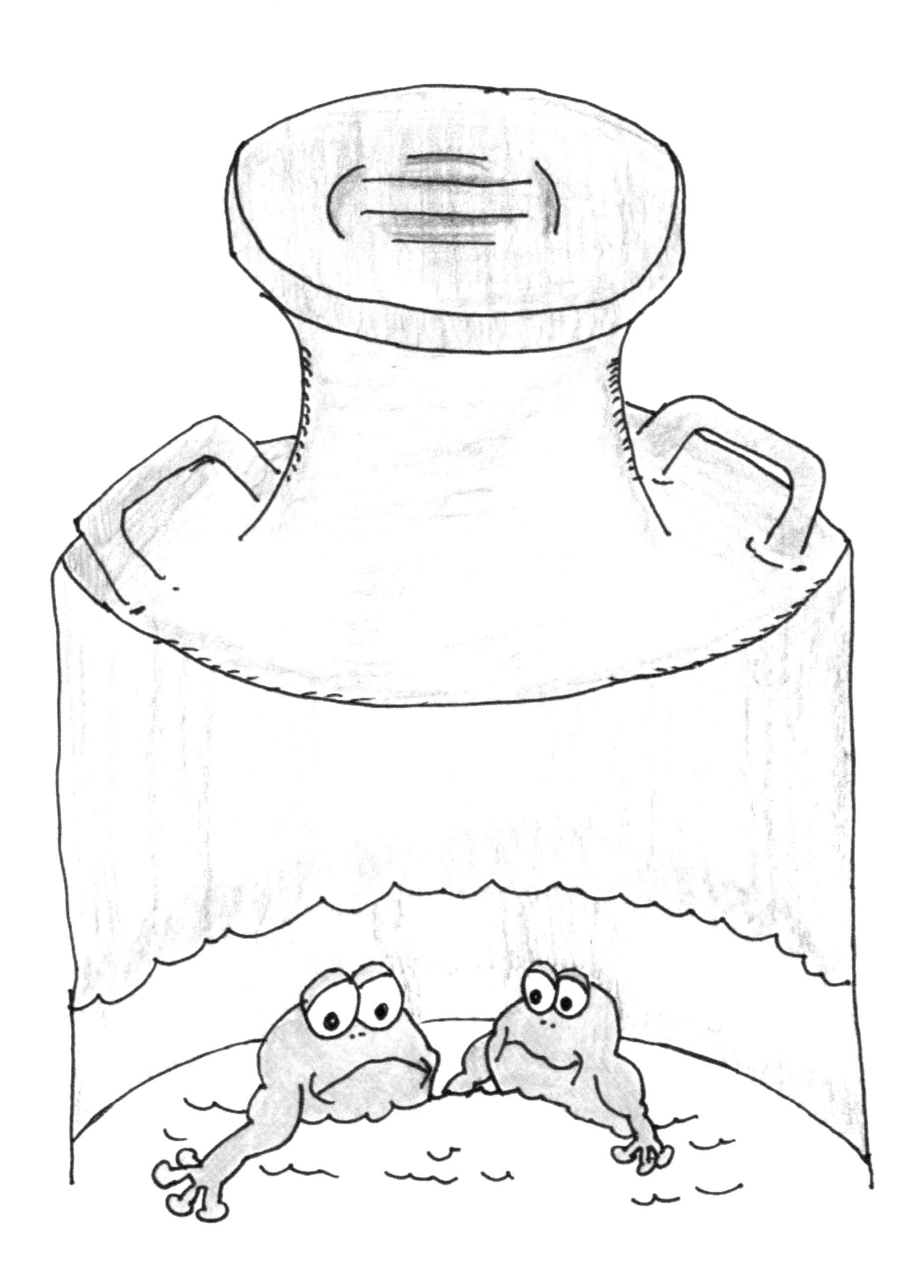

The luckless frogs began to quake,

and sober up on cold milk shake.

They find that soon their breath will stop,

unless they swim upon the top.

And so they kick and swim,

and swim and kick, until their weary eyes

grow dim.

Then gasping says one weary sport,
"Say old boy, no more kicks I've got.
I's not raised on a cold milk diet."

"Tut, tut the other frog cried,
A frog's not dead, until he dies."

"Keep on kicking, that's my plan.
We may yet see outside this can."

"No use. No use."
Faith heart replies,
turns up his toes
and gently dies.

The other frog undauntless still,
keeps on kicking with a right good will.

Until with joy to great to utter,

he finds he's churned a lump of butter.

And climbing on that chunk of grease,

he floats about with greatest ease.

Now, when times get hard
and you may frown,

don't get discouraged, and go
down!

Keep on kicking, no murmur uttered!
One more kick may bring your butter.

It's time to keep on kicking!

When facing life's difficulties,
put your hope in the fact, God has a prize
ahead for you. Keep on kicking until it arrives.
- A frogs paraphrase of Philippians 4:3-4

Printed in the United States
by Baker & Taylor Publisher Services